A BUSINESS APPROACH TO SUCCULENT FARMING

Complete Entrepreneurial Step By Step Guide To Succulent Garden From Scratch

ZHURI HART

DISCLAIMER

This book is intended to provide general information and insights on adopting a business approach to farming. The content within is based on the author's knowledge and experiences up to the date of publication. It is essential to recognize that the field of agriculture is dynamic, influenced by various factors such as market conditions, climate, and regulatory changes.

Readers are advised to conduct thorough research, seek professional advice, and consider their unique circumstances before implementing any strategies or practices discussed in this book. The author and publisher disclaim any responsibility for the accuracy, completeness, or suitability of the information provided. The book is not a substitute for professional advice, and the author and publisher shall not be liable for any damages or losses arising from the use or reliance on the information presented herein.

Individual results may vary, and success in farming enterprises is contingent upon numerous variables. The author encourages readers to consult with relevant experts, agricultural extension services, and legal or financial professionals to tailor strategies to their specific needs and local conditions.

This book is not intended to be a comprehensive guide to all aspects of farming, and readers should exercise their judgment and discretion in applying the principles discussed. The author and publisher do not endorse any specific products, services, or companies mentioned in this book unless explicitly stated.

By reading this book, the reader acknowledges and accepts the inherent uncertainties in agricultural endeavors and agrees to use the information at their own risk.

TABLE OF CONTENTS

ABOUT THE BOOK

"A Business Approach to Succulent Farming" offers a thorough manual for business owners wishing to enter this horticulture field, addressing the growing interest and financial potential in the succulent market. The book starts by outlining the rationale for taking a business-oriented approach to succulent farming, highlighting the growing appeal of succulents and the distinctive prospects that come with this movement.

The book covers the essentials, educating readers on the nuances of succulents, their various traits, and the environmental variables that affect their growth.

In addition, the book delves into market analysis and trends, giving readers a comprehensive understanding of the workings of the succulent market, present sales patterns, and methods for recognizing and focusing on particular customer categories.

Beyond theory, the book provides helpful advice on organizing and running a profitable succulent business.

This entails drafting a thorough business plan that includes financial predictions, operational specifics, marketing strategies, and market research. The book also offers helpful guidance on starting a succulent farm, addressing topics like choosing a location, designing the farm, choosing plant kinds, and cultivating methods.

To ensure healthy succulent growth, cultivation and maintenance techniques are covered in great detail, with a focus on water management, insect control, and propagation techniques. A separate chapter highlights the value of sustainable and organic operations, outlining the advantages of organic certification as well as environmentally friendly farming techniques.

Most importantly, the book discusses the vital topic of branding and marketing succulents, providing guidance on developing a unique brand identity, coming up with winning marketing plans, and using social media and online channels to expand reach. Due care is given to financial management and budgeting, including helpful advice on starting costs, planning operational expenses, setting prices, and keeping track of finances.

Additionally, the book foresees and tackles issues that succulent farmers may have, including methods for resolving issues and tactics for fostering resilience inside the company. The last chapters provide viewers with a forward-looking view of the sector by examining new developments in succulent farming and the incorporation of technological advancements in agriculture. To successfully traverse the difficulties of this expanding business, "A Business Approach to Succulent Farming" provides a combination of theoretical insights and practical advice, making it an invaluable resource for anybody hoping to get into the succulent market.

CHAPTER ONE

SUCCULENT FARMING INTRODUCTION

THE INCREASING ADORATION OF SUCCULENTS

Succulents have seen a sharp increase in popularity recently, showing up everywhere—in gardens, homes, and social media feeds. Succulents are tough and adaptive plants that come from arid places. They are distinguished by their succulent leaves and capacity to hold water. Plant aficionados throughout the world have been enthralled by their distinctive and varied appearances, which range from the eye-catching rosettes of Echeverias to the spiky appeal of Agaves. Succulents are becoming a symbol of modern aesthetics and environmentally conscious living because of the growing trend of incorporating these plants into office environments, wedding bouquets, and interior décor.

The hashtag trend for succulents has been greatly aided by social media sites like Pinterest and Instagram.

Because they are so aesthetically pleasing and attractive, succulents are a great topic for popular hashtags and well-curated feeds. Consequently, a flourishing virtual community has arisen, disseminating advice on maintenance, methods of growth, and creative approaches to exhibiting succulents. Succulent aficionados have developed a sense of community as a result of this virtual knowledge sharing, which adds to the perennial appeal of these low-maintenance plants.

Succulents are becoming more and more common beyond their aesthetic appeal because of their alleged health advantages. Taking care of these hardy plants is frequently regarded as a mindfulness exercise, offering people a calming and fulfilling pastime. Furthermore, some succulent types' ability to filter the air adds even more allure, supporting the rising trend of sustainable and health-conscious living. The popularity of succulents is not just a fad; rather, it represents a cultural movement that encourages a closer relationship between people and the natural world by bringing nature into daily environments.

WHY SELECT A COMMERCIAL STRATEGY FOR SUCCULENT FARMING?

People are starting to consider the possibility of succulent farming as a successful business due to the growing demand for succulents, which has sparked entrepreneurial endeavors. Succulent farming, in contrast to traditional agriculture, provides a distinct niche market with an emphasis on specialist plants that appeal to both private and business clientele. Succulents may be grown in a variety of climates because of their versatility and minimal water requirements, which increases the possibility of profitable economic endeavors.

Entrepreneurs can take advantage of the increased interest in indoor and outdoor plant aesthetics by venturing into the developing green sector through succulent farming. Starting a succulent-focused business enables diversification because these plants can be sold as eco-friendly gifts, wedding favors, event decorations, and ornamental elements in addition to decorative aspects. Due to their adaptability, succulents allow business owners to investigate several avenues for profit within the plant industry, resulting in the development of a viable and dynamic business plan.

Succulent farming also fits well with the growing focus on locally sourced and sustainable goods. Succulents can be grown in a controlled setting, which facilitates resource management, minimizes environmental effects, and satisfies a base of ethical customers. In addition to satisfying consumer demand for these fashionable plants, eco-friendly succulent farming techniques allow company owners to support the larger drive towards sustainable agriculture and ethical business practices. Essentially, taking a business approach to succulent farming is a way to get involved in a developing sector of the economy that places a high value on environmental awareness and aesthetic appeal. It's also a financially rewarding venture.

CHAPTER TWO

COMPREHENDING SUCCULENTS

DEFINITION AND FEATURES OF SUCCULENT PLANTS

The ability of succulents, a broad collection of plants, to retain water in their leaves, stems, or roots allows them to flourish in dry, arid climates. Succulents are distinguished by their ability to store water in their tissues, which is why they frequently have thick, meaty leaves or bloated stems.

The word "succulent" comes from the Latin word "sucus," which means juice or sap, emphasizing the ability of the plant to hold onto moisture. Succulents come in a variety of shapes, sizes, and colors and are members of several different botanical families.

Succulents' ability to adapt to difficult environments is one of their distinguishing traits. They thrive in conditions with little rainfall thanks to their capacity to store water, which makes them ideal for desert areas.

Succulents have also evolved several defense mechanisms against water loss, including specialized leaf structures and distinct photosynthetic pathways. These characteristics help them to withstand harsh environments and make them a fascinating collection of plants for both gardeners and enthusiasts.

POPULAR SUCCULENT TYPES

There are several well-liked varieties of succulents, and each has special qualities that appeal to plant lovers. Echeverias are some of the most sought-after succulents because of their leaf clusters that resemble rosettes. Another well-known kind is aloe vera, which has thick, prickly leaves and is well-known for its medical qualities. One member of the colorful and hardy Crassula family is the Jade Plant, which is known for its vivid green foliage. Succulents are also attractive because of their unusual shapes (Haworthias, for example) and vibrant colors (Sedums), which provide a variety of options for individuals who want to include these plants in their collections.

ENVIRONMENTAL FACTORS AND REQUIREMENTS FOR GROWTH

In addition to their distinctive morphological characteristics, succulents have become more and more popular due to their low maintenance needs. Well-draining soil is ideal for these plants because it keeps them from becoming soggy, which can cause root rot. The majority of succulents prefer bright, indirect light, and adequate sunshine is essential. Even though they can tolerate dry spells, constant watering is essential; how often you water them will depend on the particular succulent species and the surrounding circumstances. While certain types of succulents may tolerate lower temperatures, most succulents thrive in warm areas.

THE MARKET ATTRACTION OF SUCCULENTS

Succulents are popular in the market for reasons other than their environmental tolerance. They are popular options for interior and outdoor ornamentation due to their visually arresting forms and vivid hues. Succulents are frequently used as decorative accents in homes and workplaces, as well as in gardens and terrariums. They are perfect for urban gardening and small spaces because they can grow well in tiny containers. Additionally, the ease of propagation and the growing interest in collecting succulents are factors in their broad availability in nurseries and online markets.

Succulents are an intriguing class of plants distinguished by their ability to hold onto water, variety of features, and wide appeal. Succulents are an essential component of horticulture and design because of their distinctive shapes, low maintenance needs, and aesthetic appeal. Succulents are loved by both customers and plant aficionados.

CHAPTER THREE

TRENDS AND MARKET ANALYSIS

SYNOPSIS OF THE SUCCULENT INDUSTRY

In recent years, the succulent market has grown remarkably and grown to be a major participant in the worldwide horticulture business. Due to its diverse range of shapes, colors, and low-maintenance needs, succulents have drawn interest from people all around the world. This market includes a wide variety of succulent species, including less well-known types like Echeveria and Aloe Vera. Succulents are a favorite of both novice and experienced plant lovers due to their durability as well as their exquisite aesthetic appeal.

Succulent market dynamics are impacted by urbanization, shifting customer choices, and a growing focus on sustainable living, among other things. Succulents have made a name for themselves thanks to the growing trend of incorporating nature into urban settings and the spike in interest in indoor gardening and green living spaces.

PRESENT SUCCULENT SALES TRENDS

Succulent sales are observing dynamic patterns in the current market, which are reflective of changing consumer choices and behaviors. The growth of e-commerce has had a major influence on distribution routes, as growers and customers are now connected through e-commerce.

Offering aficionados an easy option to acquire a wide variety of succulents, the trend of curated succulent subscription boxes and online markets focusing on rare or exotic types has gained hold.

In addition, there's a growing trend toward distinctive and visually appealing succulent containers, which adds to the market appeal overall. Consumers who care about the environment are placing a greater value on eco-friendly products and sustainable packaging, which is consistent with the general trend toward responsible consumerism.

FINDING THE RIGHT TARGET MARKETS

Determining the target markets for succulents entails knowing the psychographics, behavioral trends, and demographics of possible buyers. Urban residents are an important market since succulents grow well indoors and take up little room, making them ideal for smaller living spaces. Furthermore, the younger generation—millennials and Gen Z, in particular—has demonstrated a strong interest in succulents due to their desire for unusual and visually striking plants on Instagram.

The need for visually appealing and low-maintenance vegetation is growing in unexplored sectors such as educational institutions, offices, and commercial venues. Strategic marketing initiatives that highlight the advantages of succulents in improving the atmosphere and air quality of indoor areas are necessary to target these markets.

EVALUATING SUPPLY AND DEMAND

Maintaining a lucrative and lasting business in the succulent market requires evaluating the dynamics of supply and demand. Growers and distributors must match their production capacities to market trends to meet the growing demand for succulents. It is essential to keep an eye on consumer tastes, stay informed about new types, and uphold high standards of quality to satisfy the market's changing needs.

Another crucial component is supply chain management, which guarantees that succulents get to customers in top shape. The relevance of ethical and sustainable sourcing processes is growing as customers place a higher value on openness and ethical manufacturing techniques.

CHAPTER FOUR

ORGANIZING YOUR PROFITABLE COMPANY

SETTING CLEAR BUSINESS OBJECTIVES

Any successful succulent business starts with a set of goals that are precise and well-defined. Before diving into the specifics of your project, spend some time outlining your main goals. Think about the goals you have for the near and far future. Is your goal to carve out a market niche for uncommon succulent types, or are you more concerned with offering a large selection of reasonably priced products to a larger pool of clients? Setting defined goals for your company helps you stay on track for growth and ensures that your tactics are working toward the same objectives. Your business goals should be the driving forces behind your successful venture, whether they be developing a devoted clientele, hitting a specific income target, or using environmentally friendly procedures to support sustainability initiatives.

MAKING A BUSINESS STRATEGY

Creating a thorough business plan is a crucial first step in starting your successful firm. This document outlines your company's aims, strategy, and organizational structure. It acts as a blueprint. Start by doing a thorough study of the succulent market to find trends, prospective rivals, and target audiences. Get a strong grasp of your succulent business's unique value proposition.

What makes it stand out from the competition? The operational aspects of the firm, such as where succulents are sourced, inventory control, and distribution routes, should also be included in the business strategy. A realistic view of your company's sustainability and profitability is provided by financial estimates, funding requirements, and pricing plans. A well-written business plan is a powerful instrument for steering your succulent company through several stages of development in addition to attracting investors.

SYNOPSIS

Your succulent business plan's core is succinctly but persuasively summarized in the executive summary. It is vital to communicate the most essential elements of your project clearly in this area since it is frequently the initial point of contact for possible partners, investors, or collaborators.

Give a succinct overview of your company's mission, vision, and key values from the outset. Give a brief overview of the ripe market and state the special selling features that will set your company up for success. Briefly describe your company's objectives, highlighting important dates and anticipated growth.

Talk about the important parts of your business strategy, like your financial projections, competition research, and target market. A compelling executive summary can pique stakeholders' interest and compel them to read the whole business plan to gain a deeper comprehension of your delicious venture.

ANALYSIS AND RESEARCH ON THE MARKET

Any succulent firm must comprehend the market to be successful. To determine the demand for succulents in your target area, conduct in-depth market research. Examine consumer patterns, tastes, and the mechanics of pricing. Determine who your target market is by taking their age, lifestyle, and gardening habits into account. Evaluate the competition by determining the strengths, weaknesses, and market positioning of current succulent businesses. Your product offers and marketing tactics can be shaped by the insightful information our study will bring you.

PLAN OF OPERATIONS

A clear operating plan is necessary to ensure that your succulent business runs smoothly. Describe the whole production process, including the procurement of materials and succulents as well as the cultivation, packing, and delivery steps. Indicate the facilities and equipment needed, as well as the people and expertise needed at each level. Take into account elements like quality assurance, sustainability procedures, and logistics. Create a dependable supply chain and backup strategies in case something goes wrong. A well-executed operational strategy guarantees the optimal distribution of resources and facilitates the simplification of business procedures.

MARKETING PLAN

Creating a strong marketing plan is essential to increasing sales and brand recognition. Promote your succulent business through a variety of methods, such as social media, internet platforms, and local events. To set your brand apart from the competition, clearly identify your unique selling proposition (USP). Develop a content marketing plan to highlight the aesthetic qualities and maintenance guidelines for succulents. To increase your reach, think about forming alliances with nearby garden centers or working with influencers. You may establish a strong brand presence and engage with your target audience with the aid of a well-rounded marketing strategy.

BUDGETARY ESTIMATES

Developing accurate financial forecasts is a crucial part of your business plan. Compute your initial expenditures, taking into account labor, supplies, machinery, and advertising. Using the results of your pricing strategy and market research, create a comprehensive sales estimate. Calculate your annual and monthly spending on things like rent, utilities, and office supplies. Compute your projected earnings and profit margins, considering variables such as market volatility and seasonality. These forecasts will give you a financial management roadmap, enabling you to make well-informed decisions and, if necessary, obtain funds. To maintain the financial stability of your succulent business, review and contrast your actual financial performance with your projections regularly.

CHAPTER FIVE

ORGANIZING YOUR FARM FOR SUCCULENTS

SELECTING AN APPROPRIATE LOCATION

For your succulent farm to be successful overall, choosing the ideal site is essential. Selecting a location that receives plenty of sunlight throughout the day is crucial since succulents prefer surroundings with lots of light. Most succulent species do best in an area that receives six hours or more of direct sunlight. Furthermore take into account the local climate and temperature fluctuations, since succulents do best in warmer climates and may not survive severe cold or frost. Make sure the chosen area permits enough ventilation as this is essential for preventing problems such as fungal illnesses.

PLANNING AND SETTING UP YOUR FARM

The way your succulent farm is set up and organized greatly affects how functional and eye-catching it is. Arrange succulent beds or pots to get the most out of the sun and make care simple. To provide easy access and prevent stepping on fragile plants, think about creating walkways between succulent beds. Using a raised bed or tiered design will improve water logging prevention and drainage, which will benefit your succulents in general. Furthermore, visually appealing layouts can improve the farm's aesthetic appeal and draw people in as a place for recreation and farming.

CHOOSING SUCCULENT TYPES FOR GROWING

Adding a range of varieties to your collection of succulents can diversify it and make your farm look more appealing. Think about things like growth patterns, color variations, and climatic compatibility when choosing which succulent kinds to cultivate. To create a well-rounded collection, mix easy-care and harder-to-maintain species. Popular succulent options with distinct qualities include agave, sedums, aloe, and echeverias. To guarantee that your growing efforts are successful, adjust your selection to the local climate and soil conditions. Providing the best growing circumstances for each kind you choose will be made easier if you research its particular care needs.

METHODS FOR PREPARING SOIL AND PLANTING

The development of nutrient-rich, well-draining soil is crucial to the well-being and expansion of succulent plants. To begin, mix a soil mixture of perlite, gritty sand, and potting soil—all of which drain well. Steer clear of dense, water-retaining soils since they may cause root rot. To improve fertility, think about adding organic matter to the soil. Make sure the soil surface and the root ball of the succulents are level when planting. Enough airflow is made possible and overcrowding is avoided when plants are spaced properly. Water succulents that have just been planted gently, letting the soil dry up in between applications. Establish a regular watering routine while considering the unique needs of every type of succulent in your collection.

CHAPTER SIX

TECHNIQUES FOR CULTIVATION AND MAINTENANCE

SYSTEMS FOR IRRIGATION AND WATERING

To cultivate and maintain plants, especially succulents, efficient irrigation and watering systems are essential. Because of their capacity to hold water, succulents need a precise balance of irrigation to flourish. While under watering may result in dehydration, overwatering might cause root rot. Watering techniques must be customized to the unique requirements of succulents as well as the environmental factors they encounter.

The "soak and dry" method is a well-liked way to water succulents. This is soaking the soil to the point of saturation, letting it dry out, and then watering it once more. This simulates the way rainfall naturally occurs in desert areas, which is where succulents are frequently found. Succulent farming frequently makes use of drip irrigation systems, which provide water straight to the base of the plants, avoiding moisture on the leaves and lowering the possibility of fungal problems.

MANAGEMENT OF PESTS AND DISEASES

Keeping diseases and pests under control is essential to keeping succulent plants healthy. Because of their meaty leaves and distinctive textures, succulents can attract a variety of pests, including mealy bugs, spider mites, and aphids. Finding early indicators of infestations requires routine inspection. Neem oil and insecticidal soaps are frequently used for pest management because they are non-toxic and cause the least amount of damage to plants.

In the cultivation of succulents, fungal diseases such as powdery mildew and root rot are also a concern. It is essential to maintain adequate air circulation and refrain from overwatering to prevent these problems. Additionally, the risk of fungal infections can be greatly decreased by utilizing well-draining soil and keeping the growth area clean. It's critical to remove diseased plant portions from a succulent collection as soon as possible to stop the spread of disease.

METHODS OF PROPAGATION

An essential component of growing succulents is propagation, which enables cultivators to share plants with others and increase the size of their collections. Succulents can be propagated by offsets, stem cuttings, and leaf cuttings. With leaf cuttings, a healthy leaf is cut off of the parent plant and given the chance to root and grow into a new plant. To grow new plants, stem cuttings from the main stem or lateral branches can be obtained and rooted.

At the base of mature succulents sprout tiny, genetically identical shoots called offsets, sometimes referred to as pups or babies. To start new plants, carefully separate them and plant them. Different succulent species require different propagation methods, thus it's important to find and use the best approach for each kind of succulent.

THE BEST METHODS FOR DEVELOPING SUCCULENTS HEALTHILY

Succulents need to be grown according to a few recommended practices to have the best possible growth and vitality. First and foremost, it's important to provide the proper soil mix; sand or perlite-enriched, well-draining soil is typically advised. Succulents require a lot of sunlight since they prefer bright, indirect light. To avoid sunburn, it is recommended to gradually acclimate them to more sunshine.

Growers can swiftly address difficulties by routinely monitoring for symptoms of stress, such as color changes or atypical growth patterns. Healthy development is supported by fertilizing sparingly during the growing season and not fertilizing during the winter when succulents are normally dormant.

CHAPTER SEVEN

ORGANIC AND SUSTAINABLE METHODS
THE VALUE OF SUSTAINABLE AGRICULTURE

An important paradigm for addressing the pressing need to strike a balance between agricultural operations and environmental protection is sustainable farming. The capacity of sustainable farming to advance social justice, economic viability, and long-term ecological balance makes it significant.

Sustainable farming prioritizes preserving the quality of the soil, water, and biodiversity in contrast to conventional agricultural practices, which have the potential to deplete natural resources and damage ecosystems. Sustainable farming tries to ensure the productivity and resilience of agricultural systems while minimizing the adverse effects on the environment through the use of techniques like crop rotation, cover cropping, and integrated pest management.

PUTTING GREEN PRACTICES INTO PRACTICE

Among the most important steps in reducing the negative impacts of human activity on the environment is the adoption of environmentally sustainable techniques in the field of agriculture. Reducing the use of artificial fertilizers and pesticides, switching to water-efficient irrigation techniques, and maximizing energy use are all examples of eco-friendly farming practices. Farmers that implement these techniques improve the general health of ecosystems, lower pollution levels, and preserve natural resources. Furthermore, adopting environmentally friendly practices frequently boosts farm energy efficiency and lowers the carbon footprint connected to agricultural operations.

ADVANTAGES OF ORGANIC CERTIFICATION

Promoting and assuring the legitimacy of organic and sustainable farming methods is greatly aided by organic certification. Strict guidelines that forbid the use of artificial chemicals, genetically modified organisms (GMOs), and radiation must be followed to receive organic certification. By following organic farming principles, which put soil health, biodiversity, and animal welfare first, producers are guaranteed to follow the certification process. Beyond just protecting the environment, organic certification has advantages since more and more people are choosing organic products because they believe they are healthier and contain less pesticide residue and more nutrients.

The financial benefits of organic certification are also very significant. Farmers benefit from a competitive advantage in the market since organic products frequently fetch higher prices. As a differentiator in the market, the certification draws customers who are prepared to pay more for goods made with socially and environmentally conscious methods. Furthermore, by encouraging sustainable farming methods that are advantageous to farmers as well as their communities, organic farming supports local economies.

The ideas of eco-friendly activities, organic certification, and sustainable farming are interconnected and contribute to the planet's general health. Because it takes a comprehensive approach to agriculture, taking into account social, economic, and ecological concerns, sustainable farming is important. The use of environmentally friendly practices is crucial in mitigating the environmental impact of agriculture. Meanwhile, the marketability and authenticity of products derived from sustainable and organic agricultural methods are guaranteed by organic certification. When combined, these ideas provide a strong foundation for developing an agricultural system that is both ecologically conscientious and more robust.

CHAPTER EIGHT

PROMOTING AND LABELING YOUR SUCCULENT PRODUCTS

DEVELOPING A DISTINCTIVE BRAND IDENTITY

In the highly competitive succulent industry, creating a unique brand identity is essential. Start by outlining your succulent business's mission and key beliefs. Think about what makes your collection different from others, such as an emphasis on uncommon species, environmentally friendly methods, or a distinctive visual style.

Create a distinctive and eye-catching logo that embodies these principles, and make sure that colors and images are used consistently in all marketing collateral. In addition to helping to create a distinctive image, a consistent brand identity encourages customer loyalty and trust.

FORMULATING A SUCCESSFUL MARKETING PLAN

Effective marketing of your succulent brand requires a well-planned strategy. Determine who your target audience is and what interests them before anything else. Write a captivating story about your succulents that highlights their beauty, adaptability, and low upkeep. To reach a larger audience, use a combination of traditional and digital marketing methods, such as email campaigns, print advertisements, and search engine optimization (SEO). To increase your reach, think about cooperating with gardening blogs or influencers. To remain current and interesting, evaluate and modify your marketing campaigns regularly in response to consumer input and industry developments.

SOCIAL MEDIA AND ONLINE PLATFORMS UTILIZATION

Having a strong online presence is essential in the digital age. Make a visually appealing and easy-to-use website to highlight your collection of succulents, featuring crisp photos and thorough information. Use social media sites like Face book, Pinterest, and Instagram to interact with your audience and present your succulents in an eye-catching way. Create a content calendar with a variety of entries that cover topics such as caring for succulents, behind-the-scenes looks, and product highlights. Feature consumer images or hold contests to promote user-generated content. Reach prospective consumers with customized ads, and keep an eye on social media statistics to continuously improve your online approach.

DEVELOPING CONNECTIONS WITH NURSERIES AND RETAILERS

Working together with merchants and nurseries is a smart approach to make your succulents more visible and accessible. Find possible partners who share the same values as your target market and brand. Create persuasive presentations and sales materials to introduce retailers to your succulent collection, highlighting its special qualities and advantages. Create partnerships that will benefit both parties by providing retailers with discounts, special products, or promotional materials. To guarantee that shops are informed about your succulents and can create a great customer experience, offer thorough training and assistance. Maintain regular contact with your retail partners, ask for their input, and modify your strategy as necessary to efficiently meet market expectations. Developing trusting connections with merchants expands your distribution network and helps your succulent brand succeed as a whole.

CHAPTER NINE

BUDGETING AND FINANCIAL MANAGEMENT

STARTUP EXPENSES AND ORIGINAL CAPITAL

When starting a new business, it's important to have a thorough awareness of startup expenses and the initial capital required to bring a business idea to life. Start-up costs are a broad category of expenses that include but are not restricted to, marketing, equipment, permits, legal fees, and first inventory.

Entrepreneurs need to carefully evaluate these expenses to calculate the overall amount needed. Sufficient financial planning is essential during this stage since underestimating costs can put a burden on finances and make it more difficult for the business to run smoothly. Giving due regard to both fixed and variable costs guarantees a more precise estimation of the initial capital required for a prosperous beginning.

SETTING UP A BUDGET FOR OPERATING EXPENSES

Any business's capacity to remain viable depends on its ability to effectively manage operating costs. Allotting money to pay for regular expenses like rent, utilities, salaries, and supplies is part of creating an operating expense budget. Businesses can find areas where cost-cutting initiatives can be adopted without sacrificing operational efficiency by creating a precise and realistic budget. A budget that is regularly reviewed and updated allows for flexibility in response to shifting market conditions. Effective budgeting helps companies set realistic financial targets and effectively distribute resources, which promotes long-term stability and growth. It also aids in cost control.

PROFIT MARGINS AND PRICING STRATEGIES

The foundation of a company's financial success is the establishment of a strong pricing strategy. The best price for a product or service is determined by several aspects that entrepreneurs must take into account, such as competition pricing, market demand, and production expenses. It's crucial to strike the correct balance between bringing in business and keeping a healthy profit margin. Too high of a price could turn away potential clients, while too low of a price could cause financial difficulties. It is essential to regularly review pricing strategies in light of cost and market fluctuations to maintain profitability and adjust to the ever-changing business environment.

MAINTAINING FINANCIAL RECORDS

An essential component of efficient financial management is keeping accurate and current financial records. It entails methodically keeping track of earnings, outlays, and other financial transactions. Establishing sound record-keeping procedures not only makes it easier to comply with legal requirements but also offers insightful information about the company's financial situation. This data is the basis for well-informed decision-making, tax planning, and performance assessment.

Modern accounting software makes record-keeping easier, lowers the possibility of mistakes, and makes sure that financial data is readily available for reporting and analysis. Maintaining accurate and thorough financial records is essential to accountability and transparency, which are critical components of developing stakeholder trust and long-term company success.

CHAPTER TEN

OBSTACLES AND REMEDIES IN SUCCULENT AGRICULTURE

TYPICAL OBSTACLES SUCCULENT FARMERS FACE

Despite its widespread acceptance and increasing demand, succulent gardening is not without its difficulties. Succulents' vulnerability to pests and diseases is one major barrier. Even though they are resilient, infestations can still spread swiftly and wipe out a whole crop. Succulents also frequently encounter issues with drainage and soil quality. A major issue that compromises the health and vitality of succulents is root rot, which can be caused by improper soil conditions.

A further difficulty in cultivating succulents is the requirement for ideal weather. Certain conditions are ideal for succulents, and changes in humidity, temperature, or amount of sunshine can affect how well they develop.

Unsuitable weather patterns can cause plants to grow slowly, bloom poorly, or even die. Moreover, it might be difficult to maintain a consistent revenue stream and market presence due to market swings and rivalry among succulent producers.

METHODS FOR SOLVING PROBLEMS

Succulent farmers can use a variety of ways to problem-solve to overcome these issues. To control insect populations without endangering the environment, integrated pest management is a comprehensive approach that combines biological control, cultural activities, and the cautious application of pesticides. Farmers should also take strong measures to stop the spread of illness, like cleaning tools and equipment regularly to reduce the chance of contamination.

To counteract problems like root rot, it is essential to improve drainage and soil quality. Farmers can improve the structure and water-retention capacity of their soil by adding organic matter. Proper drainage can also be achieved by utilizing well-draining potting mixes or implementing raised beds. Additionally, you can shield succulents from harsh weather by making an investment in weather-resistant structures like greenhouses or shade netting.

Succulent producers should concentrate on broadening their product offerings to overcome market obstacles. To draw clients, this might entail trying out several succulent kinds, introducing distinctive arrangements, or even providing instructive classes. Stabilizing market presence and opening up new distribution channels can also be achieved by cultivating strong ties with nearby stores, landscapers, and nurseries.

DEVELOPING BUSINESS RESILIENCE

Succulent farming requires a blend of adaptation and strategic planning to build resilience. Investing in research and development is essential if you want to keep up with the most recent advancements in pest control, cultivation strategies, and market trends. Attending workshops and working with agricultural specialists regularly can help farmers stay ahead of difficulties and get valuable insights.

Furthermore, a succulent farming business's long-term survival can be improved by implementing ecologically friendly and sustainable procedures. This could involve using less chemical inputs, conserving water through effective irrigation systems, and using organic fertilizers. Sustainable agricultural methods appeal to environmentally concerned consumers while also helping to conserve the environment.

Another resilience tactic is to establish a strong internet presence. Succulent growers can expand their consumer base and reach a larger audience by implementing social media platforms, creating an easy-to-use website, and turning their business into an online store. In addition to helping with product marketing, this online presence provides a forum for knowledge exchange and networking with other people who share an interest in succulents.

Just like every other agricultural venture, succulent farming has its share of difficulties. However, succulent growers can overcome challenges and establish a successful, long-lasting business by using proactive techniques for problem-solving and putting an emphasis on resilience-building.